Dracopis Press

OR_ELSE_a

Poetry,
or else

Anisur Rahman

www.dracopis.com
beard@dracopis.com

Dracopis_002   OR_ELSE_a
Anisur Rahman: Poetry, or else

ISBN 978-91-87341-02-1
EUROPE. First edition.

[Also available in the USA:
ISBN 978-91-87341-04-5]

Poetry is a matter of feeling. It is not a commodity on the market. It does not care about consumers' or expert or authority opinion. It is totally up to the poet. A poet is always keen on reaching his readership. What I would like to read as a reader is poetry. As a reader, I do not need to have any logic on this. My choice is enough. The texts tell my mind what is poetry to me. It may be written by an established poet or by an unknown one. If you don't know that, you haven't read poetry. Poetry is to tell a poet's mind.

0.

The task of thinking is over, that is why one sits down to write. Everything starts from zero and it is the same in the case of writing. Try to be empty. Something will be created from the surge of emotion and flow of feeling. Just do it. Thinking is for an academic scholar. Scholars should think. Let them think how to quote and make excellent use of the technique of cut-and-paste and how to construct long lists of reference sources at the end of the text. You have a vital source of energy in you. Just make use of it. Sit at your desk every day. Have paper and pencil ready. Never stop reading.

1.

Knowledge cannot resolve your poetic problem if you do not have a poetic mind. As far as I know, many great poets dropped out, or did not care about their academic record. Rabindranath Tagore is one example. It does not mean that he was ignorant. He knew a lot and at the same time had a poetic mind. What is a poetic mind? That is another question. Many professors of poetry or literary scholars have a vast knowledge of poetry. Their knowledge does not resolve their poetic problems. If they lack a poetic mind.

2.

What is poetic mind? A mind that is desperate to lose anything but poetry. Plato excluded poets from his imaginary state. Why was he afraid of poets? Plato knew that poets do not believe in class discrimination. A poet finds human beings are equals. On the other hand, to run a state, as per Plato's ideas and my observation, discrimination is a must. A poetic mind never accepts such discrimination. A poetic mind is ready to tell the truth about the beauty of life. A literary scholar runs for office at universities without such beauty in mind. His knowledge can solve problems by writing dozens of Ph.D.'s. His mind is not a poetic one. A poet's mind is ready to say goodbye to everything for the sake of poetry. A literary scholar cannot do that.

3.

To be a poet is to be foolish, stupid. A stupid person cannot do anything good. A stupid person is not expected to achieve anything. Poetry is not necessary for the family, for society or state. Poetry has no place in the job market, in the capital market, in an election campaign, in policy making, or in a government agenda. Rather poetry-writing by any member of the family causes huge suffering in terms of finance, social status and future security. When a family faces trouble because of a poet, the society or state concerned will not stand clear from that either. In this context poetry is stupid work. That is why this stupid species of mankind has been sent to prison in many countries.

4.

To be a great poet is to be very stupid. I envy such stupidity. It is a pity I have not yet achieved such stupidity. Such stupidity entails to ignoring much lucrative work over a lifetime. What lucrative work is this—reading advertisements for jobs every morning, doing courses in management, business administration, language, technical work or trying to obtain some training that can help to earn money? Instead one begins the day by reading or writing poetry or smokes sitting on a bench or kills countless pains or pleasures in life, or passes the evening playing piano; what should I say to such a person? A great poet is truly stupid. I envy the poets. I envy stupid people. I do not think I am the poet that I always wanted to be. I am not stupid either.

5.

To fall in love with your own writing is simply suicidal for a poet. That is why a great columnist cannot be a great poet. Writing is a habit. A columnist has the habit of writing columns. Addressing many day to day issues, he earns a name and fame for himself. So he gets a lot of feedback every day. It makes him fall in love with his own columns. It encourages him to be more serious about writing. An individual who could be a great poet gets lost in writing columns. Journalism makes talented people fall in love with their own writing. In this way, journalism kills poets.

6.

Poetry is to present images in words. Poetry is to express feelings in language. Poetry is a matter of being. It is not something that one can do. Henrik Ibsen says: "Poetry is to see." Wordsworth stresses that poetry is the spontaneous overflow of powerful feelings. I would say that poetry is inner dialogue. Thus poetry is also theatrical text. This spontaneity, this seeing and this being will create such a linguistic expression that a reader will get the feeling of obtaining the sounds in music and seeing the images in paintings and the feeling of powerful surges from expressions. Poetry is not a matter of understanding. However, a poet has a responsibility, as poets are considered to be the guardians of language. What you are writing must be clear to yourself better than to anyone else. Otherwise, you have no moral right to write about it. This is the confidence and feeling you have to attain. This is the condition one must know.

7.

It is important to be an individual talent so as to create a tradition. Bengali poet Jibanananda Das made a point by saying a country hardly gets one poet every decade. Optimism does no harm. On the contrary, we see hundreds of people are writing poems. What are they? They are poets but fail to create something new. What is something new? This means to emerge as a new voice with a new approach, a bold stand as to the existing tradition of poetry in a country. From this same point of view, we see brands change their shape, label and pattern of marketing—to attract consumers. In poetry, a great poet does the same with hard work, true devotion, and serious attainment in the mastery of language, getting the images, creating a new way of making metaphors but without endangering spontaneity.

8.

Poetry is not like showbiz. When the Swedish poet Tomas Tranströmer publishes a book at roughly ten-year intervals, there is no danger in him. On the other hand, there is danger, I guess, in that a comic performance poet or poetry slam master stagnates. In Bangladesh, many a poor guy publishes rubbish in literary supplements every year without engendering a lot of interest in the minds of readers. One should feel sorry for them and for the foolish illiterate literary editors. Talking to my friends in other countries, I have learnt that even they are not free from this illiterate phenomenon in the media in the name of poetry. It is a good thing to take a year writing a poem, rather than writing hundreds of pieces of rubbish.

9.

Experiment is important for attaining one's own poetic approach. The poet who does not experiment will have no way of creating his own poetic tradition. Experiment is expected when it requires spontaneity. Otherwise, poems will have no appeal. They will simply be boring texts. A committed poet knows when experiment is okay or not. Experiment is a never-ending process. It will continue to the end of every poet. It is ability in a poet. Great poets appear through great experiments.

10.

The whole process of writing is creation. It starts at the level of inspiration and ends in the final draft. Choosing refers to the use of techniques and words. While writing a poem, a poet shows his mastery when choosing words. Sometimes a poet takes the liberty of playing with words or creating new forms of words, changing the position in the syntactic process in poetry. This is also creation. When a weak poet does the task, it sounds irritating. When a great poet does the same, it sounds musical. We can quote Allen Ginsberg as once he was asked by a poet friend, "What is the plural form of poetry?"—"Poetry has no plural form, but if you need you can make 'poetries', it is all right in your case."

11.

It is the ultimate goal of a poet to break conventions. This is a poet's luck. This is the rebellion in a poet. A poet who no longer can break loose from convention is to be pitied. Then existing poems are enough. It is somehow like a market condition. Producers must study the psyche of the consumers, so must the poet. Readers do not like to accept the poems by a new poet on the strength of old conventions. The poet concerned may learn from the existing conventions. He should break them. People in poetry slam claim to make provocations. I see that they can be successful as comedians or clowns, entertaining the audience somehow. Provocation lies between painful and painless contradiction.

12.

Poetry is an outcome of rebellion. When frustrated, poetry is the beautiful shelter to create such rebellion. Frustration helps to fuel this. T. S. Eliot began with frustration. As poetry is an outcome of spontaneous overflow of powerful feelings, there are many ways for a poet to get inspiration. Life is the first and last school for a poet. Love dominates this school. It is good to begin with that. Love helps you find similes and metaphors easily. To begin with imitating a favourite poet also helps one to get into the world of poetry. Later on, a committed individual will necessarily create his or her own realm.

13.

A poet is not like an obedient bureaucrat. Obedience helps a bureaucrat to get promotions. Disobedience helps a poet to gain status. Provocation is an integral part of poetry. This is the ultimate spirit of writing. When a poet praises something good and beautiful, it is an indirect provocation to something bad and ugly. Most great poets somehow revolt in order to create their own tradition. But, to be a decisive rebel is not always good when writing poetry. It is political or propagandist when it misses the spontaneous requirement for the poem concerned.

14.

Why do so many people have such a hard time understanding poetry? Because poetry is not something to understand but to feel. Poetry is not like the stock market. Poetry is not cricket or football. It has to be felt. Something is wrong when you try to understand poetry. When some people say they do not understand poetry, they are lying. They in fact do not read poetry. They are the true enemies of poetry, but the same people usually do not say they do not understand the Quran or the Bible or the Tripitaka or the Guru Granth Sahib.

15.

Why does everyone have an opinion about poetry?
Because, everyone has at one time wished to be a
poet. In fact, everyone is a poet at one stage. Even
a professional killer tries to find metaphors for his
beloved while making love or dating. The moment
makes him a poet, true poet. Politicians necessarily
try to make their speeches poetic. Journalists do
the same when making journalistic pieces. In the
mind a thief draws the poetic outline for stealing.
Falling in love makes one a poet. One tries to send
a poetic line to a lover. A president killing women
and children in the world, I guess, does not forget
to give a poetic kiss to his wife or some metaphors
while making love with her. No problem, wel-
come everyone. If Adolf Hitler, George W. Bush, or
Osama bin Laden had poetic minds and attempted
to write poems, there is nothing wrong with that.
The question is whether those were to be poems
or not. A notorious person who has poetic talent
can separate the two entities: notoriety and poetry.
As with Ezra Pound, who became a supporter of
Mussolini.

16.

Poetry reminds bureaucrats to serve the promotion of beauty in public life. Dictators are afraid of poetry, thinking it may be the cause of revolution. The power and spiritual values in poetry can never be counted. But, it matters a lot in life. When Allen Ginsberg wrote a poem called "Jessore Road", addressing the mass killing in Bangladesh by the Pakistani occupation army, patronised by the U.S. authority in 1971, poetry mattered much. And Bangladesh's national poet Kazi Nazrul Islam was imprisoned for many years, because of his poem "Bidrohi" (The Rebel) against the British colonial occupation. Poetry matters a lot. Bangladesh and India have chosen poems from Rabindranath Tagore as their national anthems. I do not agree with the Zimbabwean poet Chenjerai Hove, who says poetry is a weak existence. I think he is confused. Poetry is a shelter to life. Poetry is a disturbing element to the upholder of the unjust. Yes, poetry matters, but not always the poet.

17.

A poet is biased towards truth, beauty and life. If I do not find something is beautiful, I could do something else. So do capitalists, bankers, bureaucrats, soldiers, propaganda machine politicians, and extremists who make deals against humanity. I find beauty in the nobility of Nelson Mandela, difficulties of implementation of good will in Obama, a lion heart in Mahatma Gandhi, Martin Luther King, Dag Hammarskjöld, Bangabandhu Sheikh Mujibur Rahman and Olof Palme. I find something beautiful in the caricature of a good many prime ministers today, whose poses remind us that they show themselves up as corporate bosses but lack statesmanship. And I am biased towards love. I find spirituality over beauty in kissing. This is me, and I find something beautiful despite all my angers.

18.

To be a poet is to be sovereign. Poetry is the highest form of sovereign thinking. A poet does not care about any certificate, any academy, any university, any media, any authority, any dictator. First he cares about a reader in him, and then he cares about a critic in him. This critic is active until he thinks a poem is printable. A poet talks to many, even to master poets, about poetry. But, for his own poetry he is the ultimate and only independent authority. He may have orientation in many ways, but he is ultimately the decision-maker about his own poetry. He always remembers that nobody can make him a poet but himself. It is not a gift. It is an outcome of one's devotion. When you decide to be a poet, you decide to be independent. "Poets are jumping frogs," as the Bengali poet Rafiq Azad manifested in a comment to the Indian poet Shankha Ghosh.

19.

Writing is a habit. Writing is a practice. While practicing, mistakes are to be expected. No learning is free from mistakes. If you do not see the mistakes in your writings, then you are to be pitied. Poets are not prophets. They do not carry divine messages from the gods, but tell their minds and learn from life. Life requires mistakes. Otherwise life is not real. Mistakes help a poet progress and therefore gain confidence. Perfect writings are idle and useless. If a footballer or cricketer can make mistakes, why not a poet?

You do not have to go to writing school to be a poet. But, you must have an orientation. If you can have it by other means, why should you be in school? Many great poets are dropouts from academia. Academia has no such depth. In many countries there are still no creative writing schools or writing courses. But there are many great writers. Without having a degree in agriculture, one can be a very successful farmer; without studying commerce one can be a successful businessman. But, they have practical knowledge in agriculture and business. That is important. In fact, no art can be taught. Only one thing can be achieved from education in art or writing and that is inspiration. It somehow also guides you on how you can be oriented yourself. Teaching can help you become a good reader of poetry. But most teachers of literature, from elementary to university levels, do not know what poetry is. They know some grand theories. Poetry does not follow any theory. They know some important names. Poetry does not care about such important names either. Art or poetry is a matter of being self-taught. If I need to find a teacher I always find bad poets, though I learnt a lot from good poets. Shakespeare had no teacher, Henrik Ibsen had no teacher, Rabindranath Tagore had no teacher. So what? They were teachers to themselves.

When you are afraid of losing ideas, it may be that you lack ideas. Writing is a matter of sharing ideas. Do you think if Shakespeare's ideas of sonnets were given to someone else, that this person could write such sonnets? It never happens. One should take writing seriously. It is not such a romantic activity that you would take pen and paper and sit at the table to write sonnets. You need to know how to craft that sonnet. You need to know the craft of poetry. Writing is craftsmanship. Craftsmanship is a part of orientation. Without orientation, you cannot presume to be a poet. This is true for every work and every art form. One must know how to do it. Otherwise, despite having many prospects, a poet may get lost.

Priority is the taste of a reader. A great poet is a great reader first. A poem will not be irritating to your ears when you read it aloud. You will get natural musicality in it and rhythm as well. It does not matter whether you have knowledge of music or rhymes. Your ears are a testing instrument. You will know it very well. You have no right to confuse your readers. You can only do this if you are very confused or not honest with yourself. By inviting confusion in writing and committing dishonest practices in writing, you ultimately kill yourself. A poet must be committed to life, but to nothing else. A poet knows that he is working with the right things. Otherwise, he can be warned. Entertainment must not be priority. I am not dismissing the importance of entertainment. But it will come through enlightenment. Do not be guided by the actors who are enjoying an authoritarian position with regard to poetry events or publishers. You may be misguided, confused or irritated. Respect them only if they are truly serious readers of poetry or if they themselves are also committed poets at the same time.

23.

To promote my poetry is important: as important as sending my daughter to school. If I cannot reach my readers, there is no point in writing. The promotion of poetry is a must. It also makes it easier for a poet to survive when writing. Survival is always a must. When you cannot survive, writing or art is simply meaningless. It is like scientific discovery: If it is not promoted and does not reach people, it has no life-enhancing role. To me, to promote poetry is also to promote life. There are ways to reach readers. The best way is bilateral reading. The poet will read and the other one will listen. I mean a poet's humble and easy communication with the reader who truly loves his or her poems. Public readings, magazines, and published books can help to have such bilateral listeners over coffee or wine. But, be sure not to disturb the existing love. A committed poet needs to be serious to make his or her presence.

24.

A poet has no way of being self-critical. He is aware enough while writing and printing. A poet's thinking is sovereign in the extreme. When he allows his poems to be printed, that's it. To be self-critical is simply a weakness in a poet. It is not expected. It is not appreciated. Before publishing a poem, a poet thinks about it a thousand times, whether it is printable or not. Literary editors are also playing the role as gatekeepers, if they are not too illiterate. A poet should not have time to be self-critical. Rather, he can invest that time in reading or writing something new.

A poet cannot always write good poems. Not all poets can write good poems. Some poets write bad poems but are continuously published. Some poets write good poems, but are not published so often. When making art, an artist is careful with lines and the use of colour. In the same way, a poet needs to be careful with words, themes and getting the musicality where the concepts of quality lie. Poetry is a matter of feeling. Reading is a matter of pleasure. Readers do not like to be irritated when reading a poem. That is why concepts of quality exist in poetry. Poetry tells the mind. It is not a matter of whether you are a teenager or sixty plus. You must have focus. You need to get to know the tradition of poetry in rather a short time. As a late beginner it is better not to hesitate.

Publication is also a process. After publishing a book, a poet thinks about the next one. It is also an occasion to forget poems that one has already written. It creates the basis for a new beginning. However, careless publication cannot be expected. The publication of bad poems should not be appreciated. Some poets suffer from writer's block, but are still avid to be published. That is why they continue to publish, and repeat. It is simply a poetic crime. Sometimes the senseless media insists on big names and the poets supply them old wines in new bottles. Illiterate literary editors are happy for that. They publish them. They have a permanent list of poets. They decide in advance which poet should be number one in their literary supplement and who will be last, and they even decide in advance who will not be published by any standard. This is the stupidity that prevails in the head of literary editors in different countries. That creates a basis for some poets to keep repeating. But, great poets always avoid repeating. So called slam poets have minimum ways to avoid repeating.

I prefer smaller publishers. I never forget that publishers are businessmen. First and foremost, they need to survive, then to make a profit. They are not charities. That is why they go for popular writers; they are in search of bestsellers. Nothing is wrong with this. They are businessmen, first and last. That is why a poet should prefer smaller publishing houses. There they will be much more careful for a book, even by a minor poet. A poet will easily have harmonious correspondence with that publisher. Bigger publishing houses, on the other hand, will simply offer corporate deals. That is irritating to a poet.

It is not true that you only gain recognition when you are dead. It depends on the socio-political condition of any given country. It depends on the state of freedom of thought and freedom of expression in a country. Sometimes recognition invites controversies. Who cares about recognition? The Nobel Prize is the number one recognising instrument, but not free from controversies. It fails to recognise many legendary master poets in the world. So what? A great poet does not care about recognition but readership. Ultimate recognition exists in readership. It is not a matter of whether the poet is dead or alive. All poets expects such recognition in their lifetime. But a poet, who does not know his or her limitations, may be lost someday along the line.

29.

When you are happy with your poems, it is simply suicidal for you as a poet. When you can make your readers happy, it is your success. It is not so easy. After a long effort, a poet can reach the mind of thousands of readers. Making his readers happy, a poet can have prospects. These include getting media attention, invitations for readings, prospects for getting scholarships and prizes, generous offers from publishers. True poets do not care about popularity. This does not mean that a true poet will not be popular. A poet who avoids appearing in media will miss out on chances to promote the poetry. Whether your poetry is good or bad is a secondary question. The readers will judge, in the long run. In the short run, a poet should try to appear in media with honesty. Uphold your spiritual integrity as a poet. Rich people are able to buy their way to name and fame. Many people are on such a practice in the name of charity, human rights and democracy. All these things are a fashion to them. Poetry can be a fashion in the same way.

30.

The best way to work is forgetting your shortcomings, and just continue reading and writing. Read bad poems and good poems. By reading bad poems you will build your confidence, seeing that many a people are writing rubbish in the name of poetry. That will give you a feeling that you should never write such rubbish. Reading good poems you will get a feeling of what poetry should be. You will unconsciously get into a mindset that will help you to write better. This determination will help you overcome your shortcomings. Never be dictated to by any critic. Being clear and unclear is not the concern of poetry. It matters only whether the "poems" are *poems* or not. Remember most critics are failed poets. T.S. Eliot called them slaves under the original works of others.

A poet is not an expert. A poet is not a specialist. But this does not mean that a poet will not have an idea about what he is writing. He must have his best idea first. Then he has the moral right to write it. Writing a poem about a patient or a hospital does not require a poet to specialize early on. The same can be said about poems on war, love and so. A poet learns from life. If there is any necessary specialization it lies there. A poet must be an obedient student to this school.

Poetry is a question of the spontaneous overflow of powerful feelings. Such a feeling does not always require the need of questioning. It is simply a matter of spontaneity. If it requires questioning anything particular in a poem before or while writing, it is all right. I consider my poems to be my personal politics. I find poets are a vulnerable political species in society. Society is mostly blind when it comes to knowing a poet. In other cases, people think that any individual who has nothing else to do writes poems. All this makes a poet an absent existence. Poets are not considered as any particular group for taking their poetic voice to policy making. What can a poet do? The only weapon a poet has is the power of writing. However, it requires the attainment of craftsmanship in writing. This is important. Orientation, commitment, continuation, sensitivity, voracious reading, a clear idea about what a poet writes and to be true to oneself. That is all. Poetry is autodidactic matter. A poet must know it.

33.

As a poet you only know that you will not stop reading and writing. When a passenger is travelling by air, he will reach the destination without knowing it. It is the duty of the pilot to know. As a passenger it is my duty to complete the formalities and to get into the air bus. The world of poetry is bigger than sky and sea. It is vain to try to know one's track, right or wrong. The right thing is to make a decision to continue writing. Let readers see whether I am on the right track or not. Poetry is not God's gift. One has to be a poet by one's own efforts. However, T.S. Eliot finds it a miracle in William Shakespeare and John Milton.

One has to have a sensitive mind along with poetic eyes and musical ears. Poetry is seeing. That is why eyes are important. Poetry matters in order to have musicality in language. This musicality can be judged by your ears. Keep on reading and writing to survive as a poet. The rest will come to you. A productive poet works with many methods. A poet excels himself every day, every moment. This can ensure his position in the vast seas of poetry. Bengali poet Sukanta Bhattacharya presented the full moon as "half-burnt bread". This is poetic seeing. These are poetic eyes. When Tomas Tranströmer writes, "Waking up is a parachute jump from dreams" this is seeing through poetic eyes. Poets like Sunil Gangopadhyay, Nabarun Bhattacharya, Chandrakanta Murasingh in India, Rafiq Azad and Nirmalendu Goon in Bangladesh, do not need to have performances to gather audience. The metaphors or images come to life in their writings.

Poetry is not just any assignment that you can decide beforehand. It is like fishing in the immensity of waters. Before catching a fish, you cannot say in advance that you are going to catch a particular species. The mind is always unpredictable. It is like the colours in the sky. It is unnecessary to think in advance. Sometimes you will have no control over your mind. This is a good feeling in the poet. When you can feel like that, you have a chance to be a poet. If there is anything else more meaningful than poetry to you, you have hardly any chance to be a poet. To be a poet is to be foolish.

36.

To be a poet is not necessarily to be happy. If you have reasons to be happy, you can try other things. A poet who tries to be happy, tries to kill himself as a poet. A river is happy for getting lost in the sea. For this it has to flow nonstop. It has to have a flow of water. There is battering and shattering in the heart of a river. The opposite is the death of a river, then it has no flow, no water, no pain, it simply dies. A poet has to have his pain to cash in on the making of poetry. Echoing Henrik Ibsen, I would like to say, a poet always fights against the devil eternally in him.

Poetry is not something like sport or business or politics. Poetry is a love letter to our time. Poetry is reflection on life. There is no way to generalise or compare poets in the olden days, today and in the future. What matters is the tradition and individual talent. We find many great poets in the olden days as well as today. And it is expected new poets will emerge with a new voice. Nothing can be said in advance about what tomorrow's poets will be like. Poets are not alien beings. It depends on how the future turns out. However, they must be rooted in their respective traditions, lands, languages and cultures. These are the basics in poetry, and so will be in the future. They will be part of a social and cultural trend. Let's wait to see what the trend looks like.

Poetry is not like cooking. If it would be so, every family could have a poet. There is no book which can make you a poet. First I try to listen to what others say about poetry. If there is anything confusing in their sayings, I point it out and make my observations afterwards. I do not care who agrees or disagrees. This is the boldness of a poet. This is sovereign thinking in a poet. I am always at the centre and even sometimes I try to arrive at the periphery to create dramatic sequences. Does a poet care about any suggestion from a friend or a relative when making his poetry? No. Poetry is not a matter of consensus or getting orders from anyone else. Poetry itself is a matter of autocracy. A poet is an extreme dictator when making poetry. Poetry is not democratic. A poet is not the Speaker in Parliament or the moderator in a debate.

Society must support all types of art and poetry. It will enrich tradition as well as enlighten society. The bureaucratic pattern is always in favour of normal poetry. Bureaucracy, and sometimes academia, behaves like a lame or blind animal in this question. This is a pity. They talk about freedom of expression, but they do not know what it is. Freedom of thought is a totally unpredictable thing to them. The media is also confused in many cases. How much of what you read in the newspapers about poetry can you trust? Do I need to bother to find out? I do not bother if they do not seriously endanger the development of literary spectrum. I do not count on them in the making of my own poetry. When they write something which is not confusing, I feel they are not illiterate or nonsense. When they write something confusing, I simply pity them. You can find many a stupid person in the pages of newspapers in many countries.

A true poet is always honest to his colleagues. He offers them friendly appreciation. He provides them with honest advice. He ensures amicable cooperation. He will therefore contribute towards creating an excellent literary circle. It will help him to get due return whenever he needs it. He will have much cause to be inspired by his colleagues. He will attain friendship and trust among his colleagues. Wonderful things can take place, and he has a good chance of being loved by someone else. That could be exciting. It happened in the past in case of many poets, such as the Bengali poet Shamsur Rahman.

41.

Appreciating specific poetry is a matter of personal choice, and so is the choice of poets. I do not like certain poets and a certain kind of poets. As a reader I have a right to say what I like or dislike. A poet has no right to irritate a reader with his bad poems. The reader has the right to throw away a collection of bad poems. I am always on the readers' side and I happily throw away such rubbish sometimes, but not until I've read it. That irritating reading, I do usually not as a reader but as a poet.

It is not important for a poet to comment on bad poems. After reading bad poems he will realise that he should not write such poems. A poet should comment on bad poems only when he is asked, otherwise not. As an individual, a poet has no right to undermine a person. It is his right if someone really writes bad poems. Undue appreciation is as harmful to a poet as to the literary tradition. Unfortunately, the media encourages this practice. A good poem will sooner or later get due appreciation from readers, defying the wrong approach from the media or literary critics or academic authority. A poet does not bother with such things but keeps on writing and reading.

As we know, writing is a love letter to time. Life is a school for a poet. Poetry tells the mind. Despite many texts are considered to be classics, they are not the tales of minds today. The legendary great poets did not have the experience in life that I have today. Life is a continuous process, so is poetry. A writer's complete works are a travelogue of his life. The journey started at birth and ends in death. The travelogue starts with the first poem and ends with the last poem or any other literary work. Be confident, it is important for a budding poet.

A poet always leads an absent life in the race of meeting life. A poet is alone in a crowd of millions. A poet converses with many even in his extreme solitude. A poet is usually in exile even in his homeland. What does a poet mean by success? Does he mean obtaining recognition, winning prizes, earning money, having cars, homes, a happy family? The questions are not dismissed. We have examples of poets who have all these successes. We have also opposite examples, as many got lost in exile. Even prison is a chance for a poet. Conditions include a poet's very close touch with his own language, culture, land and life. If one can meet all the conditions, then it is okay. Sometimes, a poet's personal failure in practical life is success to the world, which can be said in the case of the Swedish writer August Strindberg. A sea can never meet its hunger, nor a poet. A poet is an ever-unhappy existence, and success is mostly untouched.

45.

Never stop reading. Make reading an everyday habit. Make writing an everyday habit. Never make yourself a careerist but a poet. Never be satisfied with the knowledge you have. One needs not to learn more than others do. Try always to learn better than you did before. A poet always competes against himself. A poet needs to overtake himself at every moment. And does not need to overtake Shakespeare. Reading and more reading helps one to avoid repetition. Repetition gives the readers reason to misunderstand and underestimate you. They will also share their irritation with others. Repetition is a permanent loss. The ultimate dream of a poet is to expect his poetry to be eternal. He has nothing to do against it, but continuing reading and writing.